The Crazy Dog
Guide to
Lifetime Happiness

The Crazy Dog Guide to Lifetime Happiness

by Brian Browne Walker

WITH ILLUSTRATIONS BY Harry Briggs

A DELL TRADE PAPERBACK

This book is dedicated to my father

The author plans to donate a portion of his proceeds from the book to Native American rights organizations.

Published by
Dell Publishing
a division of
Bantam Doubleday Dell Publishing Group, Inc.
666 Fifth Avenue
New York, New York 10103

Designed by Sheree Goodman

ISBN: 0-440-50361-2

Printed in the United States of America
Published simultaneously in Canada
February 1991
10 9 8 7 6 5 4 3 2 1

Greetings!

THIS is not a large or a complicated book, but the idea at its heart is a powerful one indeed. It is a principle both simple and profound, and it is this: To be more aware is to be happier.

What do I mean by "more aware"? I mean, simply, more tuned in: more conscious of yourself, your thoughts and feelings, your actions and inactions, the issues and events of your life, and all the people, things, sounds, movements, and currents around you.

Think about your reveries, those times when you become so absorbed in an activity, like watching a child or making love or doing work that you care deeply about, that you completely lose yourself in it. I believe that what distinguishes these moments from other, more run-of-the-mill experiences in life is the quality of awareness and attentiveness that you bring to them. You are nowhere else but *there:* utterly concentrated and focused, thinking of nothing else, quiet in your mind and open in your heart.

You can teach yourself to be aware and focused in this way just as surely as you can teach yourself how to make breakfast or drive a car. This book will show you how to use some very simple practices to calm and center and heal yourself into a dramatically increased awareness of your life — and into the very genuine, walking-around, day-to-day happiness that accompanies it.

About the Title

THE inspiration for the title of this book comes from a Crow Indian practice. When they felt that their lives had fallen into a rut, the Crow used to engage in what they called Crazy Dog Activities. It meant just what you might imagine: They dressed in ridiculous outfits, stayed up all night banging on pots and singing nonsensical songs, ate breakfast for dinner and dinner for breakfast, and did just about everything they could upside down and backward. They did all this to wake up, to make life fresh again, to find new beauty and teachings in the places in life that had become stale and ordinary. The purpose of the ideas in this book is the same: to wake you up, to slow you down, to open your eyes to the beauty and wisdom and humor hiding just beneath the dusty, crusty surface of your life so that it can become vital and fresh and juicy again.

Some of the old Crow Crazy Dog Activities were pretty extreme. I won't be asking you to take off your clothes and tie a bright scarf over your face and ride a big white horse downhill as fast as you can go until you fall off; you probably wouldn't go along with it, anyway. But I am going to ask you to spend a few minutes a day doing some modern-day Crazy Dog Activities, and they have the same objective as the old ones: to slow you down and focus your awareness so that you can see and feel and comprehend the movements of the great river that is your life.

Using This Book

THESE essays are brief. They are meant to be read in just a few minutes, but they're also meant to stay with you throughout the day. The idea is to practice the day's activity for a while, stop when you're tired of it, think about it again a little later, and so on. It's hard to do that if you don't remember the activity, so I've designed the book to help you do that.

Opposite each essay is an illustration designed to capture the essence of that day's Crazy Dog Activity. Put the book where you'll see the picture often during the day: on your desk if you work in an office, on the kitchen counter if you're a homemaker, wherever you're most likely to see it again and again. The point is to keep the picture in front of your real eye so that you keep the idea in your mind's eye. And do one activity every day for a month or so. If you use the book this way, you'll get a lot more out of it.

A Note About the Use of the Word "God"

YOU will see the word "God" from time to time in this book. I use it because it works for me in capturing the essence of a very high ideal, but I encourage you to substitute any word or phrase that works better for you. Others that have been suggested are "my higher self," "love," "the greatest good," "the universe," and "the great and powerful Oz." In the end I believe they are one and the same. Use the one that suits you best.

My Promise to You

HERE are thirty-five Crazy Dog Activities. They are simple, but they are powerful. If you practice them, they will stop the world and open your eyes and reveal wisdom and beauty where before you've seen only pain and aggravation.

Turn the page and begin doing them, one a day, today. If you don't want to begin at the beginning, don't. This isn't school, but if it were, *you,* not *I,* would be the teacher. So start at the end and work backward, if you like, or start at the middle and work in circles, or just go at it any old Crazy Dog way you want. If you relax and do one a day for a month or so, I promise that you'll find yourself feeling happier and more alive. *Hoka hey!*

The Crazy Dog
Guide to
Lifetime Happiness

Ready? Set? Stop!

THAT'S right, stop: before we can begin, first we must stop. Before quietness can begin, first busyness must stop. Before relaxation can begin, first tension must stop. Before happiness can begin, first the roots of unhappiness must be seen.

Today's Crazy Dog Activity is a simple sitting meditation. Here's what you do:

1. Sit down in a quiet place (the way Crazy Dog is sitting if you can, but it's okay if you need to use a chair).
2. Close your eyes, gently straighten your back, and breathe deeply through your nose, filling first your stomach and then the area of your heart. Pause for a moment; then exhale softly through your nose.
3. Watch and listen to your mind.

The point is simply to observe your mind, without the distractions of sight or sound, and to learn something about its nature. If you're like most people, your brain will go just a little bit crazy: speeding up, creating images and feelings like boredom or perhaps curiosity or anger. That's okay. Whatever happens, *just watch.*

If you'll do this a couple of times a day for five or ten or fifteen minutes, you'll begin to see something. (The longer you sit, the more revealing this practice is, but do what feels right and what you have time for.) Just by observing and beginning to understand the nature of your mind, you begin to slow it down a little, to quiet it, to empty it of unnecessary thoughts. You will begin to understand how full your mind is and how busily it works to keep itself occupied. By slowing down the noise, you make space for calm and quiet and happiness to come in.

So sit, breathe, watch, listen. And remember, don't worry about what happens or judge it in any way. Just watch your mind, listen, and learn. This is the way to happiness.

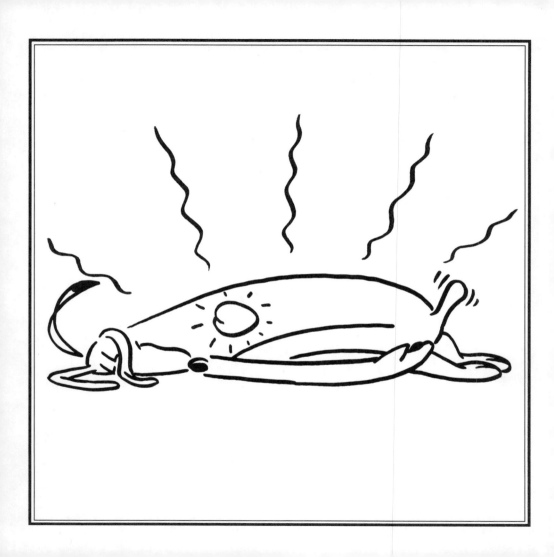

Breathe into Your Heart

MODERN science is discovering today what yogis have known for thousands of years: that the human heart is not just a muscle but also an intelligent gland. It secretes important chemicals that control the higher functions of the brain. When it's working well, we think and feel better. Today's Crazy Dog Activity is to breathe into your heart, focusing your attention there, expanding your heart energy, and releasing your body's best juices.

If you can, lie in the child's pose, as Crazy Dog does. This simple pose gently stretches your spine and releases calming chemicals into your bloodstream. (Try it before you get out of bed in the morning; there's no better way for your body to begin the day.) Close your eyes, breathe deeply but softly through your nose, and simply see and feel your breath enter and exit your body through your heart.

Allow your heart to expand and be cleansed with each breath. Wherever you feel tightness or darkness in your heart, consciously release it and breathe a feeling of love into the place where it was. As you feel this love building, turn it loose — love yourself, love this moment — and feel your best energies expand outward from your heart into the rest of your mind and body and on out into the world.

This is a great meditation to do anytime, anywhere. You don't have to be lying down, and you don't have to close your eyes. You can do it when you're chopping vegetables or walking your dog or working (one of the very best places!). Just breathe in love, let it expand and fill your heart, and breathe out all your worries, anxieties, and concerns. This is the way to happiness.

Burn It Up

NEGATIVE thoughts and emotions will burn *you* up if you don't burn *them* up. Slow down for a moment and think about the hours and days you've spent being angry at someone, or depressed, or feeling sorry for yourself. It's satisfying in its way, isn't it? It gives us a genuine thrill to feel these strong emotions. But what did it ever get you? Nothing in the end, but more anger, more depression, more self-pity.

Here is a Crazy Dog Activity to get negative energy out of your life — not to put it on a back shelf or pretend that it doesn't exist, but to acknowledge it and then burn it up in order to make room for positive energy and happy emotions. It takes only a minute, and it works.

Get a candle, and go into a draftless room where you won't be disturbed for a few minutes. (It can even be the bathroom, and if you don't have a candle, use a lighter — though a candle is nice because you don't have to hold it. If you don't have either, *imagine* the flame; it works just fine.) Light the candle, and make yourself comfortable with the flame twelve to eighteen inches from your face.

Breathe softly and deeply through your nose, and focus your awareness on the flame. Shut everything else out and actively search for all the negative energy you can find in your life: anger at someone in your family, bore-

dom with work, frustration about your finances — anything that feels bad. Whatever arises, use your focused awareness to funnel that feeling right into the white-hot center of the flame. Don't worry about replacing it with anything; just concentrate on feeding it into the fire and burning it up.

See and feel every negative emotion in your life consumed in the white heat of the flame. When you can't think of anything else that's making you unhappy, you're finished. Take a moment or two to breathe deeply and feel how you've cleansed yourself, and then blow out the candle. This is the way to happiness.

Precision Dog Following

THOUGH this is not, by appearances, a scientific book, I am going to reveal here a new theory that is sure to revolutionize biological and evolutionary thinking. It is, simply, this: Dogs are smarter than human beings. And I can prove it, using the time-honored method of comparison and contrast.

Consider these facts: Dogs lie in the sun all day, scratching lazily and rolling in fresh grass; they are fed, housed, bathed, and given loving attention by their owners; they can stay up late, howling at the moon, anytime they darn well feel like it. In exchange for these privileges they do ... well, very little, other than informal public service activities like chasing their tails to amuse small children.

Humans, on the other hand, rise at ridiculous hours to shrill alarms, put on neckties and hard shoes, and spend their days shuffling around in offices lit by harsh fluorescent bulbs, staring grumpily at buzzing computer screens, and arguing with other irate humans on the telephone. At the end of the day, they drive home through traffic; pay the rent, phone, utility, insurance, automobile, credit card, and grocery bills; eat microwave dinners; and fall asleep to the incessant badgering of television commercials, only to rise the next day and repeat the ritual — stopping, of course, to feed the dog on the way out the door. See what I mean?

Today's Crazy Dog Activity is precision dog following. The instructions are simple:

1. Locate a dog, either your own or someone else's. It is not necessary that you be on a first-name basis with the animal.
2. Introduce yourself politely to the dog.
3. Follow him around for a while.

Although you are likely to learn quite a few things, don't set out with any particular agenda. Just quiet your mind, loosen your collar, and follow the dog around. Remember, don't walk him, let him walk you.

Whatever direction he wants to go, go that way. Whatever pace he chooses, adopt it. If he stops to sniff the garbage, you stop, too (sniffing is optional). If he decides a nap is in order, stretch out nearby and snooze. You shouldn't be so much imitating him as watching him for clues to how to live happily.

This is a most restful and entertaining practice that can be enjoyed by virtually anyone. I recommend precision dog following to all my friends as an effective remedy for the stresses and strains of late-twentieth-century life. It's mighty peaceful, and golly, that sun feels good on your coat. This is the way to happiness.

The Bear in the Bushes Is Actually the Ice-Cream Man

DO you remember how as a child you could see a giant bear crouching in the bushes where you walked at night? Can you remember how terribly frightened you became, waiting for him to spring out and get you? And can you remember what a relief it was to discover — when you finally worked up the courage to take a closer look at that bear — that the bear was merely an old log or a shadow? Well, adult life is just the same, except that, up close, the bear in the bushes is actually the ice-cream man.

The bears that frighten us as adults are our problems — unrewarding work, strife in a relationship, financial difficulties. We see them as barriers to our happiness, something we'd rather sneak around or turn back from than face head-on. But that's exactly backward. If something in your life is troubling you enough to seem like a problem — to seem like a bear in the bushes — then facing and coming to terms with *that very thing* is the next step for you in achieving true happiness. The key is to go right to the bear — calmly and gently, but with the resolve to meet him head-on and find out what he has to say to you. More often than not, you'll discover he's waiting

not to spring on you but to give you a treat: an increase in your understanding of an important issue in your life.

Today's Crazy Dog Activity is to pick just one problem in your life and to go into the bushes to confront the bear. Whatever is bothering you most, focus your awareness on that. Think up all the questions you can about this situation, write them down, and then really consider them, one by one, until you feel the "problem" beginning to unlock.

If you hate your job, ask yourself, Why am I having such a bad experience at my work? Is it because I don't love myself enough and I'm using my job to make myself feel bad? Is the work itself inherently unsatisfying? If so, what kind of work would really stimulate me, and how can I go about getting it? Or does my current job actually have the potential to be challenging and rewarding if I throw myself into it more wholeheartedly? And don't forget to ask the ultimate question: What lesson am I teaching myself with this situation?

When you gently — but with perseverance — look into the heart of a problem, you will find a teaching that you need to learn before you can be truly happy. Just as with shadows, the longer you look in, the more you will see. So today be a Crazy Dog and go into the bushes. Talk to the bear until he turns into the ice-cream man and offers you a treat. This is the way to happiness.

Live Today for When You're Eighty

THIS is the simplest of Crazy Dog Activities, but if you really adopt it and begin to practice it, it's also one of the most powerful. This is all there is to it: In every decision you make today — which food to eat, how to treat someone you're having a bad time with, how much or how hard to work or play or argue or love — consider how it's going to make you feel when you're eighty.

Is is lunchtime? Slow down, breathe, focus your awareness: How will that steak and french fries affect you when you're eighty? Will your health be compromised then by what you're eating now? Is there something else you can eat that will make you smarter and calmer and healthier when you're eighty?

What about that person you're having words with? Do you want to remember yourself as someone who stubbornly yelled and fought and bickered to the bitter, ugly end? Or would you rather look back with the satisfaction of knowing that you strove to forgive and love others and to lead the way in healing damaged relationships — even when you didn't always feel like it?

What about the work you're doing? When you're eighty, are you going to say, "I became the man or woman I wanted to be," or are you going to say, "Well, I never quite got off the ground"? *Now* is the time to ensure that your memories in old age are proud and happy ones.

You can apply this practice to absolutely anything, large questions or small, and learn to see every time what the right, true, honest, good thing to do is. Ask yourself, What can *I* do *today* that I'll remember proudly when I'm eighty? This is the way to happiness.

Lasso Your Own Happiness

JUST as a cowboy lassoes a horse, so we "lasso" states of mind. Most people spend a great deal of time anticipating and dreading the negative things they believe are about to happen to them: sickness, lack of money, trouble at work, frustration in a relationship. If you think about it, your ability to imagine these things is quite astounding. You can see and feel and hear every sniffle, every moment of fatigue, every word of an argument.

When you do that, you're throwing a lasso around this negative thing and pulling it right to you. You're announcing, "This particular unhappiness belongs to me" — and soon it does! Today's Crazy Dog Activity is a simple exercise that teaches you to lasso happiness instead of negativity.

Pick a positive state of mind or event or way of being. It can be as general or as specific as you like. You might elect "happiness" or "harmony" or "complete calm," or you might choose something quite precise: "a loving relationship with Kathryn" or "a first-class woodshop where I can make fine things for a living."

Sit somewhere quiet for a few minutes and close your eyes. Take a moment to deepen and relax your breath, and then begin to see this positive thing in your mind's eye. If it is "happiness," see a happy place. Is it outdoors or in? What is the weather like? What does it smell and sound like

there? Now place yourself in the middle of the scene. Feel the physical feelings that you imagine you would feel there. Imagine the temperature and how you are moving or resting your body. Are you singing or swimming or making love? Can you feel a gentle breeze through the fine hair on your skin? Allow yourself to come fully into this place and feel all the feelings associated with it.

When you have done this, throw a golden lasso around it. See the lasso fall over it and close, and see the rope draw taut. Feel how the lasso connects you to this happy thing.

Now take a moment to relax and enjoy the fact that something good is on its way to you. Understand that you've asked to have happiness in your life. As you do this, see yourself clearly in the new, positive condition, and then open your eyes and go on about your business.

Don't worry about what is going to happen or when. You have lassoed a piece of your own happiness, and it is on its way to you. This is the way to happiness.

That Ain't Music
At All—or Is It?

DO you know people who listen to the same five records they loved in high school—and nothing else? Or people who listen to the same radio station all the time—and nothing else? I do, and I reckon that's as good for your brain as eating hamburgers at every meal would be for your stomach.

Today's Crazy Dog Activity is to listen to some music that's different— *wildly* different—from what you usually listen to, and to listen to it carefully rather than casually. Don't just switch radio stations while you're driving to work (although you can do that, too; every new perspective opens your life up a little bit more). What I suggest is this:

Go to a good independent record store, browse around looking at things you wouldn't ordinarily dream of buying, and buy one. You might want to consult with the clerk about albums he or she thinks are particularly noteworthy, but don't be afraid to pick one because you like the title or the photo of the funny-looking guy on the cover. If you normally listen to American top forty music, buy a bagpipe album or some music from India. If you listen to classical music most of the time, buy a rap album and find out what is on the minds of some people you may not know so much about. If jazz is your thing, buy country; if country, then jazz. If you can't afford to buy something, don't despair. Every town's library has records to lend, so go there.

Once you've chosen your music, find a good place to listen to it uninterrupted. Close the door, turn off the phone, and find a comfortable chair. Or take your Walkman and go lie down in a field somewhere. Put on the music, close your eyes, and listen — *really* listen, actively listen, listen like there's a message in this music just for you.

Just take it in at first, whatever it sounds like, without comparing it to anything or judging it in any way. Allow yourself to develop a feel for it, however strange and unfamiliar it is. Once you have, ask yourself: What is this music about? Are these people mad, or happy, or sad? What are they trying to get me to do with this music? Change my style? Change myself? Change the world? How do I feel when I listen to this closely? How do I feel after I listen to it? Do I feel sillier, more refreshed, more relaxed, more serious? Do I feel smarter? Do I feel like I understand this music better than I did before?

The Crazy Dog mind is an open mind. Like the Crazy Dog stomach, it is hungry for different spices, different textures, different experiences. Feed it some crazy music from time to time. This is the way to happiness.

Make Note of Your Life

ONE of the most basic forms of the awareness that is necessary to happiness is awareness of how you spend your time. Most people, when asked what they did on a given day, will say something like "I don't know — worked, ate, watched TV. That's about it, I guess." If you wanted to examine that life for clues to the source of the person's happiness or unhappiness, you'd be hard pressed to come up with any solid ideas.

Today's Crazy Dog Activity is to make note of how you spend your time. The way to do it is to write down what you do today. You can put a pen and paper in your pocket and do it as you go along, stopping every hour or two to notice what you've been doing and write it down, or you can write it all down in one sitting at the end of the day. It truly doesn't take very long, and when you have it in front of you, you have a new window into your life.

The more attention you pay to detail, the more this exercise will reveal to you. You cooked breakfast? What did you cook? Whom did you cook it for, just yourself, or did you ease the start of someone else's day by cooking some for that person, too? Did you eat it fast or slow? Did you really taste every flavor, or did you just throw it down the hatch? Did you give thanks for it before you ate it?

You went to work? What did you think about on your way there? Did you stop working at any time to stretch and relax your body, or did you just go-go-go all day long? Did you read anything today? Was it worthwhile, or was it just some trash that filled up time? Who called you today? What did you talk about? Were you nice? How many times did you hug someone today? Yell at someone?

Write down everything you can remember. If you slow down and take your time, you'll be surprised at how much detail comes to the surface. When you've covered the day, take a look at what you did with this part of your life. Do you notice anything about how you're spending your time that makes you especially happy or unhappy? Can you do a little more or a little less of it?

Your time is your life. Focus your awareness on it today. This is the way to happiness.

Be Bigger Than You Are

No one is nearly as "small" a person as he or she thinks. One of the greatest barriers to human happiness is the idea "I can only do so much." Today's Crazy Dog Activity is to pick an area of your life where you think that way and then *be bigger than you are:* do more and do it better than you usually do, or think you can do, or even want to do.

Is there something at work that you don't absolutely have to do or that someone else is supposed to do but isn't doing? Grab it for yourself: just jump right in, complete the task, and keep quiet about it. Is there a way to do something nicer—to make it tighter or cleaner or smoother? Go the extra mile, even if no one will notice. Do it *especially* if no one will notice, and when it's done, say to yourself, "I can do more, and it's *no problem.*"

Is someone giving you grief? Don't pay attention to how you feel about it; pay attention to how *that* person feels. Don't talk back, just listen and acknowledge his or her feelings. Take the worst he's got and then ask if there's anything else he wants to get off his chest. Open yourself up, and let it roll off you like water off a duck's back. You can take it.

Are you nice to someone once a day? Be nice to someone ten times today. Go out of your way to pay a compliment or buy someone lunch or rub the back of a neck. Prove to yourself how easy it is to be a sweetheart.

A warning: You may find this extremely pleasurable. If you do, don't worry about it. Just go ahead. Steal someone's work, relieve somebody's pain, clean a floor that isn't quite dirty yet. Be a Crazy Dog, and be bigger than you are. This is the way to happiness.

29

Try Something New

WHAT'S troubling you in your life? Pick three things that really bother you, things about which you have concrete judgments: "He was a jerk, and he owes me an apology, and that's that"; "My work is boring — always was, always will be"; "*I'm* not cleaning up after them again; they just don't care about me." And here is today's Crazy Dog Activity: Suspend all your judgments and try something new.

Think about it. If these things have been bothering you for a while, *whatever you've been doing and thinking about them isn't working.* More yelling and arguing aren't likely to break that relationship through to bliss. More cynicism about your job isn't going to make it open up into a nine-to-five wonderland. Whatever it is, if it's still vexing you, then your old attitudes and behaviors aren't transforming it, so transform them.

Imagine your life as a windshield. You know it won't get cleaner if you pick at the bugs one by one, rubbing a little spot here and there with the dirty old rag of judgment. So for today switch on the washers and wipers full blast. Turn the hose on your life, and let it rain; wipe your view of this person or job or situation completely clean.

Forgive someone who doesn't deserve it. Apologize to someone who ought to apologize to you — and mean it. See the poetry in your work; see again why it's important. Give money to someone who owes you. And if you want to be really daring, try this one out: Trust that God is arranging for you to have a terrific life.

A Swedish poet named Tomas Transtömer said a wonderful thing: "You can see beauty if you look quickly to the side." Who or what in your life that is now ugly could become beautiful if you looked to the side? Today choose to look to the side and try something new. This is the way to happiness.

Love Your Crib,
Love Your Self

HAVE you ever noticed how much attention people pay to making a baby's crib and room look nice? They carefully choose little mobiles and dangling toys and soft blankets. They paint the walls lovely colors and sew new curtains and put in music boxes that play the sweetest of songs. Why do they do it? They do it because they realize that the baby's surroundings tell her who she is, how much the family loves her, what kind of world she lives in.

Well, you're a baby, too, and today's Crazy Dog Activity is to focus your awareness on the cribs you've made for yourself. Ask yourself, What does my home say about me? How does it reflect me to myself? Have I given some thought to the things I've brought into it and how I've arranged them? Does it have an abundance of light and air? Are there plants living in it and around it? Could it be more comfortable? (And don't be misled by the idea that it takes a lot of money to make a nice home; it ain't necessarily so.)

Have you chosen the things in your "crib" as if they really mattered — as if they were for a precious being who deserved a beautiful and comforting home? Is it neat and clean, the way your baby's room would be? Do you have some toys in it that stimulate your curiosity and encourage you to

think, or is it full of toys like the television set that allow you to sit passively and do nothing?

Where else do you spend a lot of time? In an office perhaps? How does it reflect you to yourself? Slow down and really take a look at it and ask that question: What do my surroundings say about me?

Today, focus your awareness on your crib. Remind yourself that *you* are a beautiful baby who deserves a nice home. Clean off a table; paint a room; wash some windows; organize your desk; add a happy color to something. Love your crib, love yourself. This is the way to happiness.

Wash That Dog,
Frolic with God

ONE of the most powerful ideas in this book — one of the ones that will change every nook and cranny of your life for the better — is on this page. So pay attention: Dog washing and dishwashing are ways of frolicking with God, if you approach them in the right spirit.

A story is in order. My big white hairy dog needed a bath one Friday evening at the end of a hectic week. I didn't want to bathe her. I knew it wasn't going to be any fun, and it wasn't. Bending over the tub made my back hurt, and it made me more tired and more grouchy. When it was over, though, I was glad to have it done — until a half hour later when she went out into the garden and did a samba through the compost heap. Bath time *again*.

What could be worse? Well, nothing — except that I decided that it wasn't going to be worse. I knew the evening was going downhill unless something changed, so I decided to change my attitude.

First I slowed down, relaxed my breath, quieted my mind. Then I said to myself, "This dog isn't a pain in the neck. She's my best friend. If she's got a good enough sense of humor to dive into the muck right after a bath, I'm going to have a good enough sense of humor to jump in the tub with her and make a party of the second bath!" So that's what I did: got covered with mud and soap and wrestled with my dog and laughed until I blew bubbles from my nose. It was fun the second time around because I decided it would be.

What do you have in your life that you don't want to do? A floor to clean, a lawn to mow, papers to file? Today's Crazy Dog Activity — I dare you to be crazy enough to try it — is to pick something that makes your heart sink and your eyes glaze over and *throw* yourself into it like a dog headed for compost.

Love and happiness and unfathomable beauty are hiding inside the most mundane tasks. Have you a toilet to clean or some dishes to wash? Sink yourself into the task. Really feel the dishes in your hand and experience the sensual warmth of the soapy water. Wallow in the pleasure of turning a nasty smudge of leftovers into a shining platter fit for a king or queen (like yourself) to eat off. See how with every pass of the sponge you are caring for yourself and the people you live with.

Slow down and settle into the meditation of ordinary tasks. Be aware of your heart, and you may feel it: God is in there frolicking with you as you wash your dog or your dishes. This is the way to happiness.

God Is
in the Trees

"**N**O man is an island," said John Donne, and there can be no genuine happiness for people who aren't aware of how their lives are connected to and supported by the world around them. You have some very good friends out there doing some amazing things for you, and you may not even know who they are. Today's Crazy Dog Activity is to acknowledge and strengthen your connection to them.

Try a little experiment. Stop breathing right now, close your eyes, and count to a thousand. Hold your breath the whole time. When you get to about seventy-two, see what is at the top of your list of priorities. Go ahead, try it.

If you did, you see what I mean: The air we breathe is life itself. But how often do you contemplate and appreciate where it comes from? Slow down now, and consider that without plants and trees, the CO_2 we exhale would saturate the atmosphere and make life impossible for us. Plant life is more than pretty; it is part of your body.

Give Crazy Dog thanks and praises for your life today by adding a tree or plant to the place where you spend the most time. If you can't afford to buy a new one, make friends with one that is already there. Nourish this friend, care for it, learn about it, and see it for what it truly is: an extension of your lungs.

When you need some extra energy, stop what you're doing, go near your plant, and take some deep breaths with your eyes closed. Thank it for turning your useless old CO_2 into something fresh and clean and invigorating.

Look around you as you move through the world today. Understand just how much health and beauty and light are brought to you by your friends who wear green. Give thanks and praises: God is in the trees, and life is yours. This is the way to happiness.

Earthquake!

WHEN the Great Earthquake of 1989 came to California, I was near its epicenter at Santa Cruz. I learned that earthquakes have a fantastic way of focusing one's awareness. Today's Crazy Dog Activity is to pretend you're going to have an earthquake right where you are.

If you were about to be smashed under a building, is there anything you'd like to say to anyone first? With whom would you want to bury the hatchet? To whom would you like to pay a compliment before you die? Is there anyone you would want to meet, or thank, or hug? Do you have a bill you'd like to pay or a wrong to make right before you go? Would you want to give your all in your work today?

What if it wasn't you, but someone you know, who was about to die in an earthquake? What would you want to pass between you today? Would you want to say, "Thanks for being my friend all these years," or, "We've had some hard times, but all in all you've been a great father"? Perhaps today is the day to say that. Perhaps today is the day to buy that lunch, send those flowers, rub those shoulders.

Today, act in a way that you'd like people to remember you for eternity. And after today, don't wait for an earthquake. Be a Crazy Dog, and have one every day. This is the way to happiness.

Cast Out Worry

THERE'S something very similar about little babies and the coolest old people. Have you ever noticed what it is? They don't worry.

You, too, were born free of worry. You came into the world startled, bewildered, curious, amazed, and delighted — but worry never would have occurred to you as a baby. Whose worry have you taken on since then?

Today take a Crazy Dog look at something you worry about: money, health, your family, whatever you like to worry about most. Where did you learn to worry about that? Did your parents worry about money and teach you how? Did it ever get them — or you — any more money? Notice your worry, and cast it out of your life like dirty dishwater out a window.

Do you worry about someone in your family? Think about it. Does it genuinely help him or her — or you — in any way? Cast out worry.

Do you worry about war or sickness or poverty or natural catastrophes? Does it have any effect other than to make you sick and unhappy? Cast out worry.

Do you worry that something will happen or worry that it won't? Does your worrying make the slightest bit of difference in what eventually happens? Cast out worry.

Mind you, this is not to say, "Throw up your hands and give up." This is to say, "Do all you can about the things you can do something about, and leave the rest in God's able hands."

So slow yourself down today and see what you are worrying about. Then get old, get young, get free. Cast out worry. This is the way to happiness.

Paint a Pretty Picture, Make a Beautiful Life

THINK, if you will, of your life as an art gallery and of the events in it as paintings that you have made. A week ago or a year ago or just yesterday you began a picture, and today it turns up in the gallery that is your life. You stop to look at it. Is it beautiful: "joyful marriage hug" or "belly laugh on a sunny sidewalk"? Or is it ugly: "argument at work" or "car accident"? Whatever it is, see it as a painting in the gallery of your life, and consider that the spirit in which you paint today determines how nice your gallery looks tomorrow.

Look at the pictures you've done in the past that are turning up in front of you today. Ask yourself a Crazy Dog question: What was I saying about myself when I painted this picture?

Look also at the pictures you are painting today that you're going to have to look at in the days ahead. Are you painting a "I'm grouchy, so I'm going to take it out on my family" painting today? If so, be aware that one day there will turn up in the gallery of your life a painting that has "incomplete family happiness" written all over it.

Today's Crazy Dog Activity is to paint pretty pictures. Paint a "I love my mom, so I'm giving her a hug" picture, and see what kind of relationship you have with her tomorrow. Paint a "I'm going to take the heat off someone who's swamped at work" picture, and see how your job strikes you next week. Paint a "I'm going to help clean up some part of my town" picture or a "I'm going to exercise my body" picture today, and see what kind of town and body show up in your "gallery" next week, next month, next year.

Understand, you are the source of all that happens in your life. Paint a pretty picture, make a beautiful life. This is the way to happiness.

Life Is Right

Life is right, in any case.

— *Rainer Maria Rilke*

HOW frequently does it happen that something occurs in your life that at the time you think is completely wrong — unfair, too painful, a derailment of the happy and orderly progress that you desire? Something goes "wrong" at work, something goes "wrong" in a relationship, something goes "wrong" in your body. Whatever it is, it's *definitely* wrong, and you *definitely* wish it would go away and leave you alone.

Have you ever noticed how often you discover, after some time, that this thing that once seemed so terribly "wrong" has in fact had a profoundly powerful and positive impact on your life? That being dismissed from that job — an event you thought would ruin you — in fact led to a reevaluation of your relationship to work and to a new job that made you happier? Or that the difficulty in a relationship that at first seemed so mean and unnecessary in fact exposed important issues that allowed you to have a deeper and more rewarding relationship with yourself and the other person? Or that the sickness that seemed like the last straw in fact caused you to look at your life, to change it, to move it into a place of greater calm and health and peacefulness?

Today's Crazy Dog Activity is to assume that life is right: to look at

those things in your life that you regard as bad or wrong and seize hold of the good and the beauty and the power in them.

Are you arguing relentlessly with someone? Perhaps life is teaching you to be softer, gentler, more forgiving — a course of action that will inevitably leave you happier. Are you living in a place you hate? Maybe life is asking you to form a clear idea of where you want to live and how you can get there and to love yourself enough to make it happen. You'll never go wrong loving yourself more. Is a police officer standing by your car writing out a speeding ticket? Life might be saying, "Slow down, relax, breathe deeply as you travel. Arrive rested instead of all wound up."

Today, close the gap between the time that something "wrong" happens and the time you realize that life is right. This is the way to happiness.

Crazy in My Mouf

I ONCE watched a four-year-old boy eat tapioca for the first time. It was real tapioca, the kind that looks and feels like fish eggs, and his eyes got wide when he put it in his mouth. I asked him if he liked it, and he nodded yes vigorously. "What is it you like about it?" I asked. His reply was right on the money: "It's crazy in my mouf!"

Eating is one of those places in life where we tend to fall into patterns: hamburgers on Monday night, spaghetti on Wednesday, fish on Friday, ice cream for dessert *every* night. This is no more interesting or satisfying to our bodies than listening to the same five records is to our brains. A rut is a rut is a rut. Today's Crazy Dog Activity is to jump up out of the rut by putting something crazy in your mouf.

There are lots of ways you can do this.

Eat something that's completely foreign to you — something that has a weird name, something from a distant country where people have rings in their noses, something with a texture or color or smell that's at least a little bit scary. Cook it yourself if you can — take the time to learn how to prepare something strange and exotic. When you eat it, take your time with it, inhale its scent, chew it slowly with your eyes closed and really, really taste it. Does it make your brain do a funny little dance? Good.

53

Eat only fruit one day, or only rice, or only rutabagas prepared as many different ways as you can prepare rutabagas. How do you change when you do this? Do you think different thoughts, become calmer, more troubled, funnier, more serious?

Eat at a time when you don't normally eat or in a place you don't normally eat — or better yet, both. Have your breakfast at three in the afternoon, sitting on the roof watching the world go by. Eat a plate of lasagna at six in the morning in the toolshed, or in your car. What's it like? How does lasagna taste so early in the day? How do you feel when you do this — a little crazy, a little bit more alive? Good.

Don't eat for a day. There are lots of people in the world who very often don't have the choice. Take a day to experience what they experience. You might end up sending a check to a relief organization. That's okay, too.

Eat a half hour apple. Get a nice fresh Granny Smith or MacIntosh and go somewhere quiet. Take a full half hour to eat it, and try not to think of anything while you're doing it except how it tastes, sounds, and feels.

If you don't like one of these ideas, make up your own. Get someone sexy to spoon-feed you, or eat your breakfast with your fingers, or wear a costume to the dinner table. The point is to shake it up, baby, to put something crazy in your mouf. This is the way to happiness.

54

Listen to Your Body

Y

OU may not think about it much, but you are probably aware of the sensitivity of the earth. Wherever you see the earth harmed, you hear it cry out in pain. When the air becomes polluted, rain turns to acid and trees are killed; the earth cries out. When the rain forests are felled, carbon dioxide proliferates and the atmosphere heats up until nothing can live; the earth cries out.

When the earth cries out, it wisely tells us, "Stop this, for it is harmful to all things." Today consider that your body has a wisdom similar to that of the earth. Focus your awareness on the crying out in your body, and discover what your pain is saying to you.

Take a few minutes to slow down. Sit quietly, close your eyes, and breathe deeply through your nose. Is there pain — an ache, a burning, a tightness, a "deadness" — in your body? If so, where is it? Ask your body, "Why is there pain here?"

Listen to your body. It may tell you that your lower back hurts because you drive too much and walk too little. It may say that your insides hurt because you eat wrongly or that your neck is stiff and sore because you sit at a computer all day. It may reveal that your chest feels constricted because you argue frequently with your spouse or that your head hurts because you indulge in worrying.

When you look at your pain, ask yourself a question: What is the desire behind this pain? Could it be that you want to sit less and walk more,

to let the tension pass from a relationship, to stretch or dance or take a nap or work outdoors rather than in? Ask your body what it wants you to do to care for it, to respond to it, to serve it as well as it serves you — and then do it.

When we ignore the cries of the earth, it withers and dies. When we honor the earth, it loves us and supports us. Our bodies work the same way. Understand today that your body is a glorious planet. Honor its wisdom, and flourish. This is the way to happiness.

Let God Open the Holes

HAVE you ever noticed the difference between a good driver on the free-way and a bad one? The bad driver is always trying to force things: entering where there is no room; turning abruptly; moving in fits and starts. The good driver is as fluid as melting ice: waiting for openings to appear and then smoothly moving through them. If you watch a great ballplayer, you will see the same artfulness. He never forces a play; instead, he relaxes while his teammates create openings, and then he glides through them to glory.

Today's Crazy Dog Activity is to become a smooth driver on the free-way of life. Ask yourself, Where am I trying to force something? Is there a relationship or job or opportunity that I'm trying to begin or end or alter in some way before its time? Wherever your awareness reveals a pushing or forcing, choose consciously to relax, to let go, to remain undecided and unmoving until a hole opens up that is so big you can't keep from going through it.

Try it. Shift from trying to make things happen to letting them happen. I sometimes call this collapsing onto God, but the idea is not to be lazy and do nothing about the tensions in your life. Instead, look into them with a focused awareness and willingness to be still until the proper action is per-fectly clear to you.

Relax, let go, and let God open the holes. This is the way to happiness.

I Scream, You Scream, Let's All Scream Till We Can't Scream

MANY spiritual teachers and psychotherapists believe that all forms of unhappiness and poor health are the product of unexpressed emotion. They argue that if we would only give voice to our emotions as soon as we feel them — expressing them completely without holding ourselves back in any way — we would be at peace, greeting every new moment free of emotional "baggage." It makes sense. Have you noticed how great you feel after a good cry or a deep belly laugh or a clear-the-air conversation with a friend or family member?

Today's Crazy Dog Activity is to open all the channels that need to be open for you to express your emotions: your mind, your breath, your heart, your voice. It sounds complicated, but it isn't. All you have to do is scream.

Choose the busiest intersection in town. Stand in the middle of the street and — no, no, just kidding. Grab a soft pillow, and go into a room where you can be alone for a few minutes. Take a deep, deep breath into the bottom of your stomach, cover your face with the pillow, and scream or yell just as loud as you can. Take another deep breath, and scream into the pillow again — and again and again and again. Don't stop until you feel that every emotion in your body has passed right out through your breath, through your heart, through your voice.

Think of everything in your life — or even in the world — to which you object, and scream, "NO!" Think of everyone you're mad at and scream, "I'M SO MAD AT YOU!" Think of everything and everyone that you love, and scream, "YES!" or "I LOVE YOU!" If you feel tired and sore and grouchy, scream, "I'M SICK OF BEING TIRED AND SORE AND GROUCHY!" If you feel happiness, scream, "YAHOO!"

When your brain can't think of anything else, let your body take over. If you feel a tightness in your neck or chest, scream that out. If you feel a burning in your stomach or an ache in your back, scream that out.

Scream into that pillow until every last cell in your body says, "I'm completely spent, and I don't have anything else to say." When that happens, sit quietly for a moment, and focus your awareness on how it feels to be free of repressed emotions. Cultivate this feeling in your everyday life by giving voice to your emotions. This is the way to happiness.

(NOTE: You'll be a little hoarse from this, probably, but just think of it as a nice, sexy, bedroom voice. And if anyone might overhear you — the pillow absorbs most but not every bit of the noise — let that person know beforehand that you're okay and that you're just doing an exercise.)

Needs Versus Desires

THE nature of desire is that we sometimes give it great power over us. Under its sway we eat ice cream when we need an apple, we watch TV when a walk outdoors would better serve us, we buy things that we can't afford, we race on to a new relationship when we could better heal ourselves by attending to the one at hand.

Today's Crazy Dog Activity is to identify your needs and attend to them. Think about what you need, and think about it on the level of food and water and air. What are the things you need to do to give a firm foundation to your life? Just for today, eliminate everything that looks like a desire. If you don't need to do it, don't.

Only you can decide which is which, but here are some clues from my own life. I find that I need: to feed myself reasonable amounts of healthy food; to exercise my body so that it stays fit; to stretch my body so that it stays limber; to breathe deeply into my heart so that I stay calm and centered; to actively love and be loved by the people around me; to pay some attention to my surroundings (cleaning a little, adding something nice, taking away something unpleasant); to notice the natural world (its rhythms,

its colors, its sounds and temperatures); and to work some with the sense that I'm not only making money to care for my family but also doing something that matters, that helps others, that invigorates me.

And I find that I desire: to buy things that take my attention off my life; to go places to take my attention off my life; to engage in activities that take my attention off my life; to eat lots of sweet things; to argue with people; and to be lazy with my mind and body and spirit.

What are your needs, as you see them? Make a list (the shorter, the better), and just for today attend only to those things on it. Give yourself food, water, air, work, exercise, relaxation, love. At the end of the day, even if you haven't indulged a single desire, you may be surprised at how good you feel — well cared for, well loved, well fed, well soothed.

Savor the feeling of satisfying your needs. This is the way to happiness.

Belly Soft, Life She Come Easy

HERE is a simple Crazy Dog Activity that will make room for happiness in every part of your life if you use it: Soften your belly center. (No, it's not about eating ice cream. It's about relaxing.)

Go somewhere quiet, and close your eyes for just a moment. Clench your stomach muscles tight, and hold them like that. Give it ten or twenty seconds, and then open your eyes and notice how you feel.

After a moment close your eyes again, and begin to breathe, softly but deeply, through your nose. As you do this, consciously relax the center of your body. Let your belly fill with air as you inhale, and allow it to remain soft as you exhale. Focus your awareness on your belly, breathing into its center, softening the belly and the rib cage, allowing everything to relax. After a few minutes notice again how you feel. You should be calmer, more centered, more relaxed.

Softening your belly is a practice that you can do at any time, wherever you are. You will find its relaxing and grounding effect to be very powerful. Use it in the face of stress — argument, fear, indecision — and it will calm and center you and gently guide you to the most beneficial resolution of any situation.

When your boss begins to yell, when you start to worry about money or love or sex or death, remember, belly soft, life she come easy. This is the way to happiness.

Make Everything
Meaningful

Meaninglessness inhibits the fullness of life and can, therefore,
be equated with illness; meaningfulness makes a great many
things endurable, perhaps everything.

—C. G. JUNG

WHAT do you judge to be meaningless? Housecleaning? An illness?
Time spent in traffic? Your work? Your life? Today's Crazy Dog Activity is to
regard every single thing in your life as meaningful. Consider that everything you see or hear or smell, everything that happens to you, everything
that someone says to you — each and every thing — is absolutely
meaningful.

Do you have to vacuum the house? Make it a meaningful contrast with
the good food or conversation or lovemaking you'll enjoy afterward.

Is there a feather on the sidewalk in front of you? See it as a meaningful
message of tenderness from a gentle old grandmother bird to you, and take
the tenderness deep into your heart.

Make everything you do meaningful. Consciously invest even your
most ordinary and unconscious activities with a dose of good will. As you
greet an acquaintance, smile and think, This touch of my hand on your

shoulder will keep you from having to stand in line at the bank one day, or This handshake will ensure that your children live long and happy lives.

Make everything that happens to you meaningful. If you're stuck in traffic, instead of fuming, try putting a blessing on everyone around you: "Okay, the guy in the green car gets an extra-big Christmas bonus this year; the woman in the delivery truck gets a long belly laugh when she needs it most; the boy on the motorcycle is spared an accident on a wet road one night...." Maybe it sounds silly to you, but how do you know the world doesn't work like that?

Today, make everything in your life completely meaningful. This is the way to happiness.

Forget Your Troubles and Dance

"Nordstrom had taken to dancing alone. He considered his sanity to be unblemished and his nightly dances an alternative to the torpor of calisthenics. He had chided himself of late for so perfectly living out all of his mediocre assumptions about life. The dancing was something new..."

—JIM HARRISON, *Legends of the Fall*

THERE is something common to people who live under oppression in different places around the world. Whether in Africa, South America or elsewhere, no matter how different the culture, they all engage in one common activity to a degree not experienced by most people in freer societies: dancing. If you dance, this will be no mystery to you. Dancing loosens the body, liberates the emotions, calms the mind, and invigorates the spirit. I have read that even Jesus, in one of the Gnostic Gospels, advocated dancing, saying, "He who does not dance does not know what happens."

Dancing alone is different from dancing in the company of others. Only when we are alone do we express our deepest and most closely guarded selves, wiggling the way we wiggle when no one's watching, making the

faces we make if no one's there to laugh. Today's Crazy Dog Activity is to forget your troubles and dance — alone.

Grab some music that moves you, lock the door, and go to it. Let the music get inside you and take charge of your body. If it says, "Jump!" then jump. If it says, "Shake!" then shake. If it says, "Whirl around cross-eyed with your tongue sticking out and bark like a seal!" then go ahead. No one will know, and your spirit will lighten for having done it.

Dance until you sweat, and then dance some more. Dance until your head is light and your heart is open and you can't think of anything you can't accept or anyone you don't like. Dance until you're smart and peaceful and good-natured, until you do what Jim Harrison's Nordstrom does in *Legends of the Fall*: "He began to get an inkling that the point was to be dancing in your brain all of the time...."

Forget your troubles and dance. This is the way to happiness.

What Are You Building?

IN Santa Cruz, California, a great many chimneys fell during the Great Earthquake of 1989 — and a great many didn't. I asked a stonemason there why some came down and some didn't. He looked at me as if I might be just a little bit thick, and said, "Well, buddy, the ones that are still standing are the ones that were built right in the first place."

Today's Crazy Dog Activity is to look at everything you're building in your life — whether it's a career or a relationship or a chimney — and ask yourself, Am I building anything that's going to fall on me when a spiritual or financial or physical earthquake comes?

Are you building a brick wall of anger or self-righteousness in a relationship? It's likely to fall back on you one day if you don't dismantle it now. Why not build in its place a foundation of love?

Are you building a rickety scaffold in your work life by not really caring about it? If it collapses under you, how much is it going to hurt? Why not build in its place a stone staircase of sincere effort?

What are you building with your friends, your children, your community? Something that will enhance and enrich you all or something cheap and cheesy that's going to bonk you on the head one day? What are you building in your spiritual life? A sun-washed cathedral where you slow down and live in love and kindness or a dark basement where you trip over things and shout curses, only to hear them echoing back at you?

Earthquakes of different sorts come and go all the time, if you think about it. It's just that if you build things right in the first place, you never even feel them. Be aware of what you are building. This is the way to happiness.

Do What
You Want
to Do

PEOPLE never get tired or bored or unhappy or depressed from doing what they want to do, but from doing what they don't want to do. Think about it. When was the last time you felt all bummed out from having great sex or laughing really hard? Never, that's when.

Today's Crazy Dog Activity is simply to do what you want to do, without judging yourself for it and without feeling guilty. Do you want to take the day off work and go swimming, or see three movies, or play with your dog in the sun? Do it, but follow the rules: No judgments, no guilt. If in your heart of hearts it's something you really want to do, then it's something you should do.

Have you been wanting to get to know someone and feeling bad that you haven't? Take that person to lunch. Is there something you want to get off your chest with someone? Get it off. A place you've been wanting to go to? Go there. A taste you've been wanting to taste, a smell you've been

wanting to smell, a song you've been wanting to learn to sing? Taste, smell, sing, dance, laugh, make love, be happy! Today do what you want to do.

While you're doing it, be aware. Notice what it is that you want to do. Notice how you feel when you're doing it. Think about what you're doing in your life that doesn't make you feel this way. Ask yourself a Crazy Dog question about that: How can I stop doing this and start doing what I really want to do?

If your answer is "I can't," then don't listen. Ask the question again — slow down, focus, wait for truth — because there is a better answer in there. If you really want to do something and you know that it's a good thing to do, then God has whispered the desire to do it right into your heart.

Today, please God and please yourself. Do what you want to do. This is the way to happiness.

Love God Like a Silly Puppy

TELL the truth: do you find the idea of "God" a little difficult? Are you intimidated by the possibility of an all-seeing, all-knowing disciplinarian looking sternly down on you from above? Are you made a little nervous by the notion of a wrathful fellow who speaks in a thunderous tongue and makes it rain for forty days and forty nights? I always was, but two things changed my mind.

The first was that someone suggested to me that "God" and "Good" were one and the same. Whether I believe in a bearded old man in the sky, I don't know, but I am certain that I believe in the force of good. I see it operating all the time: Sickness turns to health; laughter breaks out where tension has dwelt; flowers bloom in a warm and gentle breeze. The idea that "God equals good" makes it simple for me to believe in God.

The second thing — the one that brought me into a very easy, happy relationship with God — was taught to me by my wife before we were married. It is today's Crazy Dog Activity. "Love God," she suggested, "with the same feeling that you would have for your child or for a puppy — since that's what He is."

Of course! That *is* what God is! If God is the source of all things, then God must *be* all things: a beautiful baby; a silly puppy; a warm, ripe peach; a song of songs.

Today, understand that when something makes you happy, God is right there. God is the person you are hugging, the joke that makes you laugh, the night sky that opens your heart, the compassion you feel for one less fortunate, the Crazy Dog that chases its tail.

Love God like a silly puppy. Rub His belly; scratch Him behind the ears; throw a ball for Him; make funny faces at Him; giggle. This is the way to happiness.

Be 100 Percent Responsible

WHAT does your mind begin to do when you have a problem with someone or something in your life? If you are like most people, your mind immediately begins to assign blame. "If he hadn't done that, I could have done my job properly and this wouldn't have happened." "She started it — I didn't want to argue." Rather than look into ourselves, we assume that whatever is wrong is the fault of someone else. There are few things that are completely guaranteed to give you an unhappy life, but this is one of them.

Today's Crazy Dog Activity is to assume 100 percent of the responsibility for the presence and condition of every single thing in your life. Sure, you may be only 50 percent or 64 percent or 32 percent responsible, but how can you know? It's much simpler — and ultimately it will make you much happier — to be 100 percent responsible for everything in your life.

Is someone yelling at you? Be 100 percent responsible for this relationship. Look to see if anything you've done is wrong, and apologize for it; look to see what you can do right, and do it. (Not yelling back is always a good start.)

Are you behind at work? Don't blame someone else. Be 100 percent responsible. Concentrate; focus; work harder and happier and in a more inspired way.

Whatever appears in your life, say to yourself, "This is here because I invited it here, consciously or unconsciously." Ask yourself the most powerful question in the world: What would the man or woman I've always wanted to be do in this situation? Then do it.

Today, be 100 percent responsible for your life. This is the way to happiness.

Give It to Get It

I HAVE a friend with an interesting approach to money. Whenever he and his wife are running low, they turn to each other and say, "We need some money. We'd better go spend some." It sounds crazy, but it works for them, and I think it works because it's founded on a very solid principle: Whatever you want to get more of in life, you must first be willing to give more of.

This is a Crazy Dog Activity that works like magic: If you wish to receive it, first give it — and give it freely, with love. Today practice it specifically with money. Your assignment, in short, is this: Give money away.

Slow down and buy somebody a nice lunch today — and notice that it doesn't bankrupt you or kill you. (You get double points if you do it for someone you haven't been getting along with.)

Drop a dollar on the sidewalk here and there, and drop a blessing along with it: The person who picks this up will prosper for the rest of his days.

Send flowers to an enemy. When you pay your toll on the turnpike, pay for the guy behind you, too, and enjoy brightening the day of another human being. Slip a quarter to a kid, and don't forget to wink. Hand your best friend a twenty and say, "Do something fun with this, would you? I'd appreciate it." Then *appreciate* it.

Once you've got it working with money, try it with something else. If you feel unloved and you want more attention, try really loving someone else. If you desire a greater compensation for your work, first give more value for the paycheck you're getting. If you aren't being understood by someone, stop worrying about that for a few minutes and really understand *him* or *her:* Stand in his or her shoes; think his or her thoughts; experience his or her misfortunes; feel his or her feelings.

At the end of the day look back at your grace in giving away your money, your work, your joy in living, and your love for other people. Watch over the coming weeks as all these come back to you tenfold. Money, love, or laughter, it all works the same: Give it to get it. This is the way to happiness.

Change de Rhyddim

THE very essence of the Crazy Dog way is changing patterns. Humans are creatures of habit, and over time we develop ways of thinking and talking and living — rhythms of behavior — that narrow our vision and keep us from seeing the fresh beauty that is always popping up around us. We become so used to doing something a certain way that we never even stop to think about what pleasure might be available in doing it another way.

Sleeping is one of the things that we do this with. Most of us go to bed at about the same time, sleep for about the same amount of time and get up about the same time every single day. The only change might come on a weekend, when we stay up later or sleep in later, but we probably do *that* the same way every weekend, so it's just another rhythm.

Today's Crazy Dog Activity is to alter the beat of your sleeping rhythm. You should be creative about the way you choose to do this, but here are a few suggestions.

Close the door to your office at 2:00 P.M. and take a fifteen-minute nap instead of drinking more coffee. Plan to dream about when you were a kid climbing a tree. Don't forget to set the alarm on your watch.

Get up at 3:00 A.M. and take a long walk around your town in the middle of the night. See how different a place it is while everyone is asleep. See who *isn't* asleep, who stays up all night, working or singing or wandering around. Notice how the place *smells;* it will be very different, I promise you. When you get home, take a hot bath, and listen to how quiet your house is.

See what your mind wants to talk about in the middle of the night. If you have children, before you go back to bed, look in on them. They're beautiful, aren't they?

Sleep outside. Sleep naked. Sleep in a funny nightshirt with a little hat on and drink sassafras tea before you turn out the light.

Go to bed early and set the alarm a couple of hours early. Get up when it's still dark and read about someone you look up to; plant a seed in the quiet of the morning by imagining yourself becoming more like him or her.

Stay up all night doing something for someone else — make a gift, or clean the basement, or write a love letter. When your brain is screaming with fatigue, turn it off and go to sleep. When you wake and start it up again, it will be a different brain, changed forever for the better by your after-hours altruism.

Don't limit yourself to my suggestions. Make up your own Crazy Dog sleeping ways, and when you get used to those, make up some more. Change de rhyddim, mon, and feel your senses sharpen. This is the way to happiness.

Barking Is for Dogs

HAVE you noticed how warm and wonderful it makes you feel when a vicious dog is barking and snarling at you? How relaxed you become when you think you're about to be bitten? Actually it's *not* so wonderful, is it? What about when someone is yelling at you? Does it encourage you to smile and open your heart, to embrace that person, to seek mutual solutions and to love each other? Or does it have roughly the same effect as a barking, snarling dog, making you want to run away and protect yourself?

Barking dogs and yelling people do have the same effect. They turn people off; they close hearts; they increase tension and fear and anxiety. Today's Crazy Dog Activity is to become aware of how you bark at other people and to stop doing it.

Do you give a snarl when your spouse comes near? Snap at your children when you're not in a good mood? Growl at people you work with? How is it making them feel? There's an easy way to tell: How would it make you feel if you were on the receiving end?

Barking is for dogs. You aren't a dog. You're a valuable human being, and so is everyone else. So today — and tomorrow and the next day and the day after that — slow down and stop barking at people. If they bark at you, don't bark back. Just ask them to be gentle with you; you deserve it. This is the way to happiness.

Transitional Object Meditation

THE writer Morris Berman coined a wonderful term for those things we believe we can't be happy without. He calls them transitional objects, and the term implies that before we can make the transition to being happy and whole and content, we must first get or do or buy or experience a certain thing. It might be an object: "I'll be happy when I get a Porsche" or "Everything will be fine as soon as I can afford that new stereo." It might also be a person or an experience with a person: "I'd feel great if only he would marry me" or "All I want is to have sex with her and then I'll be content." It may even be a state of mind that we believe we must enter before we can feel right: a religious feeling we felt once before; a drug experience; a rush of romantic love.

Today's Crazy Dog Activity is to focus your awareness on the things you're using as transitional objects. What thing or event are you waiting for to become happy or whole? A marriage to take place, a "better" job, another drink, an apology from someone, a new car? Do you think you'll really be happy when it comes, or will there then be something else?

Become aware of how you place your happiness outside yourself. Do you regard it as your birthright, something that you possess and enjoy at every moment? Or do you make it dependent upon the arrival of a very specific set of conditions? Which would you prefer: to be in love with your life all the time or to put it off until you have every last little thing you ever wanted?

Today, tune into your transitional objects. If the lack of something or some person or some feeling stands between you and your wholeness, see it for what it is. Release it in your mind, and feel yourself whole and complete and peaceful as you accept where you are. This is the way to happiness.

Crazy Dogs Never Die, They Just Get Crazier

YOU haven't reached the end now; you've just come to the beginning. This book is at *its* end, but your life as a full-fledged Crazy Dog is only beginning. You see, once Crazy Dog is in your blood, it never goes away. A Crazy Dog for thirty days is a Crazy Dog for life.

Today's Crazy Dog Activity — and tomorrow's, and the day after that, and all the days after that — is to slow down, look around, and invent a Crazy Dog Activity of your very own. Find what it takes to trick your brain into seeing beauty and wisdom and happiness all around, and then do it.

You may think you don't have the imagination to do this, but you *do*. (I never thought I did until I made these up and wrote this book.) So just look at your life, and pick the first thing you see. If there's someone you don't like — an "enemy" — on the horizon, maybe you can ask yourself: What valuable lesson is my "enemy" teaching me? Perhaps that person is teaching you patience or compassion — and what is more valuable than that? There is your Crazy Dog Activity for the day. Call it "My Enemies Are My Teachers," and practice it.

Or maybe when you look, you'll see someone who's tired or hungry or sad or ill or needing groceries carried into the house. There's your Crazy Dog Activity. Give the very best of yourself to others, again and again and again — and laugh and dance and giggle your way through it.

You can do it. Slow down; breathe; focus. Let the deeper and gentler currents of your life hold you and teach you and guide you. On the days that you don't feel like making up a new Crazy Dog Activity, don't. That's why you have this book. Open it, and try something new. Love yourself silly. Listen to your body. Wash the dog. Be 100 percent responsible. Do what you want to do. Let God open the holes. Stop barking, and start being a Crazy Dog. This is the way to happiness.